# PreScripts
## Cursive Passages and Illuminations

### Poetry

CLASSICALCONVERSATIONS.COM

**MULTIMEDIA**

PreScripts Cursive Passages and Illuminations: Poetry

Created by Courtney Sanford and Jennifer Greenholt

© 2014 by Classical Conversations® MultiMedia
All rights reserved.
No part of this publication may be reproduced, stored in a retrieval system, or transmitted in any form or by any means—electronic, mechanical, photocopy, recording, or any other—without the prior permission of the publisher, except as follows: permission is granted for copies of reproducible pages to be made for use within your own family.

Published in the U.S.A. by Classical Conversations, Inc.
P.O. Box 909
West End, NC 27376

ISBN: 978-0-9851701-7-2

For ordering information, visit www.ClassicalConversationsBooks.com.
Printed in the United States of America

# PreScripts Cursive Passages and Illuminations: Poetry

The word "prescript" comes from the Latin words *prae* (meaning "before" or "in front of") plus *scribere* ("to write"). The PreScripts series from Classical Conversations MultiMedia is designed to precede—to come before—original writing. Just as we learn to speak by mimicking our parents' words, we can learn to write well by copying the words that others have written. Even though coloring, drawing, tracing, and copying are simple tasks from an adult perspective, imitation is at the heart of a classical education. Rather than resorting to mindless busywork that isolates handwriting from the rest of education, the PreScripts series is designed to complement the world of knowledge students inhabit as they mature.

## How to Use This Book

Each book in the PreScripts series combines a functional design with excellent content. The goal of *PreScripts Cursive Passages and Illuminations* is to refine the basics of cursive writing through practice with longer passages of writing. As your students gain muscle strength and coordination, they will be able to move from writing that is functional to writing that is worthy of being called an art. For this reason, this book in the PreScripts series can be used as either a consumable or a non-consumable resource. Students who still have difficulty with the cursive letters can trace over the writing in the book in the space provided, while those who are ready for a challenge can copy the passages in a separate notebook or on blank paper.

Our job as classical educators is to teach students to make the effort to be neat, but, even more so, it is to encourage them to aim higher by teaching them to write beautifully. Many schools no longer teach cursive writing, claiming that it is too difficult to master. Teaching a child to write in cursive does require diligence and patience, but it has a number of compelling benefits. Research suggests that cursive writing more effectively develops manual skill and dexterity. Cursive may also aid students struggling with dyslexia or dysgraphia because 1) capital and lowercase letters are distinct; 2) each word is one fluid movement, so the child's rhythm is not disrupted by frequent pauses; and 3) letters like "b" and "d" are more difficult to reverse.

When children are learning to write, what they study matters as much as how they study it. Parents are more likely to give up on cursive when the content seems frivolous, so Classical Conversations is pleased to offer cursive writing books that give the student plenty of practice using rich, meaningful content. With PreScripts cursive writing books, your student can become a confident writer while learning or reviewing important subject matter, such as history sentences, passages of literature, and proverbs.

---

In this book, we focus on poetry, one of the most ancient and compact forms of creative storytelling, both oral and written. The book is arranged chronologically, so as your student practices cursive he or she will gain familiarity with some of the world's greatest works of poetry, from ancient epics such as *The Iliad* and *The Aeneid* to modern classics by Eliot, Yeats, and Frost. Each poem in this book is accompanied by a miniature lesson in rhetorical devices such as metaphor, simile, and alliteration. If your student is interested in learning more about reading and writing poetry, we recommend *The Roar on the Other Side: A Guide for Student Poets* by Suzanne Rhodes (Moscow, ID: Canon Press, 2000).

As you work through this book, take time to discover the peculiar characteristics of poetry with your student. Some poems have strange structure, spelling, capitalization, or punctuation. Use this opportunity to practice accuracy, accuracy, accuracy! Rather than assuming they know how to spell a word or punctuate a sentence, your students will need to focus on the details of the task at hand. This skill will serve them well in writing as well as in subjects like mathematics.

To provide variety for your student and to enhance the fine motor skills necessary for writing, drawing lessons accompany the copy work. This book focuses on one element of illumination, an art form dating back to the classical and medieval periods, when manuscripts were written by hand and each one was treated as a valuable work of art. The word "illumination" comes from the Latin verb *illuminare*, which means "to light up." In the most luxurious manuscripts, an artist would take sheets of real gold or silver that had been beaten into extremely thin layers called "leaves," and he would incorporate the precious metals into his drawings and lettering. When light hit the gilded page, the manuscript would seem to shine with its own matching light.

In addition to the cost of materials, illuminated manuscripts required an immense investment of time and effort. A single book could take as few as two years or as many as fifty to produce. To give you a sense of an illuminated book's resulting value, one buyer in 1453 is said to have sold a small estate to pay for a single copy of Livy's *History of Rome*. King Louis XI of France not only had to pay a deposit in silver but he also had to give his personal guarantee and that of another nobleman before he was allowed to borrow a book from the Faculty of Medicine in Paris. Imagine if today's libraries were so stringent!

Although many artists were associated with monasteries, others were members of the nobility or independent craftsmen, both male and female. Their illuminations included ornate borders, miniature drawings, elaborate initial letters, and full-page images. They used lines, curves, dots, flowers, leaves, branches, animals, and people in their art—in short, all the elements of drawing. This book will teach your student to identify and illustrate key metaphors or visuals in each poem. Encourage your student to experiment with his or her artwork, not only in the space provided, which will vary, but also on a separate sheet of paper, giving a personal touch to each poem.

---

Although variety is important, the key to mastering cursive is to practice every day. For best results, set aside a specific time each day for cursive practice. You choose the pace appropriate for your child. You can assign one page a day to a beginning student or assign two to four pages a day to an older or more experienced student. A student who struggles with writing might even do half a page a day until his or her fine motor skills become stronger, working up to a page or two a day. The pace is completely up to the parent.

If you choose to do one page a day, there are enough pages for a complete school year, working on approximately four or five pages a week. If you participate in a Classical Conversations community, you can do four pages a week while your community meets, and five pages a week the rest of the school year. Older students might do two pages a day and complete two books a year. If you would like your student to memorize the poems in this book, you can read through them weekly to review or have your student do the same book twice.

## The Journey in Perspective

The key to good writing is daily practice. The key to a heart that seeks truth, beauty, and goodness is providing quality content to copy. We hope you will find both in *PreScripts Cursive Passages and Illuminations*.

The medieval scribes and artists who practiced illumination often did so in the service of the Church. As such, they believed that words, particularly sacred texts, were worthy of honor and respect, and they used their art to exalt the words they copied. Likewise, the goal of the PreScripts series is for your students to master the skills of copying and writing in the context of a biblical worldview, building on a second meaning of the word "prescript." A prescript can also mean a command, rule, or moral guideline. The Bible instructs parents to remember the commandments of God and teach them to their families.

Deuteronomy 6:6–9 reads, "And these words, which I command thee this day, shall be in thine heart: And thou shalt teach them diligently unto thy children, and shalt talk of them when thou sittest in thine house, and when thou walkest by the way, and when thou liest down, and when thou risest up. And thou shalt bind them for a sign upon thine hand, and they shall be as frontlets between thine eyes. And thou shalt write them upon the posts of thy house, and on thy gates." As this Scripture reminds us, writing, drawing, memorizing, and reciting are all forms of worship that we model for our students.

Let's get started!

For more information about the practice of illumination, the following copyright-free resources are available in e-book form.

- Bradley, John William. *Illuminated Manuscripts*. Little Books on Art. Ed. Cyril Davenport. Chicago: A.C. McClurg & Co., 1909.
- Middleton, John Henry. *Illuminated Manuscripts in Classical and Mediaeval Times*. London: C.J. Clay & Sons, 1892.
- Quaile, Edward. *Illuminated Manuscripts: Their Origin, History, and Characteristics*. Liverpool, UK: H. Young & Sons, 1897.

## *How to Draw from Photographs*

Illustration, along with fancy initial letters and elaborate borders, is another form of illuminating a manuscript. Novice artists can take their drawing skills to the next level by creating illustrations based on photographs. Photographs take a three-dimensional object and re-create it in two dimensions, so the photographer has already done part of the work for you. Here are three easy steps to help students make the most of the illustration lessons in this book:

1. Identify the basic shapes you see in the photo. Lightly sketch the basic shapes in your drawing space. Most artists use ovals and circles in this step, but you may occasionally use a triangle or other shape that dominates the composition of the photo. You may know this step as "blobbing."

2. Refine the contour lines (edges) of the shapes you see in the photo. Using a slightly darker line (either by using a softer pencil or just pressing down harder), draw in the contour lines, paying attention to all the curves and angles in the lines.

3. Identify the shades you see in the photo. Classify the shades as (1) light gray areas, (2) medium gray areas, or (3) very dark or black areas. Tilt your pencil to the side and rub it to create the shades you have identified. Ta-da!

### Excerpt from book I of *The Iliad* by Homer
(c. 8th century BC / Trans. from Greek by Alexander Pope, 1715–1720)

"Why leave we not the fatal Trojan shore,

And measure back the seas we cross'd before?

The plague destroying whom the sword would
    spare,

'Tis time to save the few remains of war.

But let some prophet, or some sacred sage,

Explore the cause of great Apollo's rage;

Or learn the wasteful vengeance to remove

By mystic dreams, for dreams descend from Jove.

If broken vows this heavy curse have laid,

Let altars smoke, and hecatombs be paid.

So Heaven, atoned, shall dying Greece restore,

*And Phoebus dart his burning shafts no more."*

**Trope used: Metonymy**—referring to something by naming a closely related

In line 3 ("The plague destroying whom the sword would spare"), Homer uses "sword" to represent the Trojan army. Imagine if Homer had said instead, "The plague destroying whom the Trojan soldiers would spare." Likely you see a graphic and literal portrayal of death—actual Trojan men killing people. When Homer uses "sword," however, the focus moves away from individual soldiers toward the instruments of war, violence, and death. Homer has used metonymy to create the exact image he wants the reader to see, without any distractions.

Drawing Practice

### Excerpt from book I of *The Aeneid* by Virgil
### (1st century BC / Trans. from Latin by John Dryden, 1697)

Arms, and the man I sing, who, forc'd by fate,

And haughty Juno's unrelenting hate,

Expell'd and exil'd, left the Trojan shore.

Long labors, both by sea and land, he bore,

And in the doubtful war, before he won

The Latian realm, and built the destin'd town;

His banish'd gods restor'd to rites divine,

And settled sure succession in his line,

From whence the race of Alban fathers come,

And the long glories of majestic Rome.

**Scheme used: Rhyme**—repeating the same consonant and vowel sound in the final emphasized syllable of a line

Dryden was a genius at translating ancient Latin. He used a rhyming format called "heroic couplets." In this format, the first two lines rhyme with each other, then the next two lines rhyme, and the pattern continues throughout. See how "fate" and "hate" and "shore" and "bore" rhyme with each other? You might remember this form from reading *The Iliad* or *The Odyssey*. Many epic poems have been translated this way.

**Nota Bene:** Ancient poets, like Homer and Virgil, did not write in heroic couplets; translators like Dryden added this feature later.

# Drawing Practice

### Excerpt from book XIII of *Beowulf* (Author unknown)
(c. AD 8th century / Trans. from Old English by Francis Barton Gummere, 1910)

Home then rode the hoary clansmen

from that merry journey, and many a youth,

on horses white, the hardy warriors,

back from the mere. Then Beowulf's glory

eager they echoed, and all averred

that from sea to sea, or south or north,

there was no other in earth's domain,

under vault of heaven, more valiant found,

of warriors none more worthy to rule!

**Scheme used: Alliteration—repeating consonant sounds, often at the beginning of words**

*Beowulf* was written in the eighth century AD. Back then, most poems were recited or performed rather than read. This often meant that the performer had to memorize the whole story! So, authors used alliteration to make their stories easier to remember. Look closely at the passage above. See how each line repeats a particular consonant? The first line repeats "h" in the words "home" and "hoary." The second repeats "m" in "merry" and "many." The third repeats "w" in "white" and "warriors," etc. This feature makes a poem much easier to memorize!

# Drawing Practice

## "*Soleasi nel mio cor* / She Ruled in Beauty O'er This Heart of Mine"
### by Francesco Petrarca (Petrarch)
(14th century / Trans. from Italian by Thomas Wentworth Higginson, 1889)

She ruled in beauty o'er this heart of mine,

A noble lady in a humble home.

And now her time for heavenly bliss has come,

'Tis I am mortal proved, and she divine.

The soul that all its blessings must resign,

And love whose light no more on earth finds

room,

Might rend the rocks with pity for their doom,

Yet none their sorrows can in words enshrine.

They weep within my heart; and ears are

deaf

Save mine alone, and I am crushed with care,

*And naught remains to me save mournful breath.*

*Assuredly but dust and shade we are.*

*Assuredly desire is blind and brief.*

*Assuredly its hope but ends in death.*

**Scheme used: Anaphora**—repeating words, phrases, or clauses at the beginning of successive sentences, clauses, or lines

Anaphora comes from the Greek meaning "a carrying up or back." It is one of the oldest poetic techniques and appears often in Old Testament biblical passages to create emphasis. It also serves as a powerful tool to amplify emotion and rhythm.

Throughout this poem, Petrarch speaks of sadness and death, pulling the reader into his mourning. Lest the reader resist, Petrarch asserts himself at the end, trapping us in his sadness with anaphora. "Assuredly, assuredly, assuredly" you cannot resist his mourning. It grabs you like the beat of a drum.

Drawing Practice

## Excerpt from "General Prologue," *The Canterbury Tales* by Geoffrey Chaucer (14th century)

Whan that Aprill with his shoures soote,

The droghte of March hath perced to the roote,

And bathed every veyne in swich licour

Of which vertu engendred is the flour;

Whan Zephirus eek with his swete breeth

Inspired hath in every holt and heeth

Tendre croppes, and the yonge sonne

Hath in the Ram his halve cours yronne,

And smale foweles maken melodye,

That slepen al the nyght with open ye

(so priketh hem nature in hir corages);

Thanne longen folk to goon on pilgrimages.

*And palmeres for to seken straunge strondes,*

*To ferne halwes, kowthe in sondry londes;*

*And specially from every shires ende*

*Of Engelond, to Caunterbury they wende*

*The holy blisful martir for to seke,*

*That hem hath holpen whan that they were seeke.*

**Scheme used: Assonance**—repeating vowel sounds in adjacent words with different consonant sounds

Chaucer uses a form of rhyme called assonance throughout this prologue by repeating vowel sounds. This is sometimes called "near rhyme" or "vowel rhyme." Look back at the line "tendre croppes, and the yonge sonne." Do you notice how the "o" sound is repeated three times? This makes the sentence flow when read aloud. By incorporating this type of rhyme, Chaucer amplifies the musical quality of the passage.

**Nota Bene:** Unless you know how to read Middle English, you should look this up on YouTube to hear it read. It sounds incredible!

Draw something that this poem makes you think of on your own paper, or move on to the next lesson.

## "Written on a Wall at Woodstock"
### by Queen Elizabeth I (c. 1553–1558)

Oh Fortune, thy wresting wavering state

Hath fraught with cares my troubled wit,

Whose witness this present prison late

Could bear, where once was joy's loan quit.

Thou causedst the guilty to be loosed

From bands where innocents were inclosed,

And caused the guiltless to be reserved,

And freed those that death had well deserved.

But all herein can be nothing wrought,

So God send to my foes all they have thought.

**Trope used: Apostrophe**—speaking to an imaginary or absent person or an abstract quality

Poets have used apostrophe for centuries to express vivid, strong emotions, because it enables them to speak to the source of their anguish or joy. In "Written on a Wall at Woodstock," Queen Elizabeth voices her pain to Fortune, who she believes has caused her sorrow.

# Drawing Practice

### Excerpt from Book 1, Canto 1 of *The Faerie Queene*
### by Edmund Spenser (1590)

A Gentle Knight was pricking on the plaine,

Ycladd in mightie armes and silver shielde,

Wherein old dints of deepe wounds did remaine,

The cruell markes of many a bloudy fielde;

Yet armes till that time did he never wield:

His angry steede did chide his foming bitt,

As much disdayning to the curbe to yield:

Full jolly knight he seemd, and faire did sitt,

As one for knightly giusts and fierce encounters fitt.

**Trope used: Onomatopoeia**—using words whose sound echoes the sense of the word

Say "pricking on the plaine" ten times fast. Hear that repetitive thumping sound? It sounds reminiscent of a gentle knight galloping softy through a field, which is what "pricking on the plaine" means! Onomatopoeia can be one of the hardest tropes to use, but when done so intentionally, it makes the poem more descriptive and vivid.

# Drawing Practice

### EXCERPT FROM "THE PASSIONATE SHEPHERD TO HIS LOVE"
### BY CHRISTOPHER MARLOWE (1599)

*Come live with me and be my love,*

*And we will all the pleasures prove*

*That Valleys, groves, hills, and fields,*

*Woods, or steepy mountain yields.*

*And we will sit upon the rocks,*

*Seeing the shepherds feed their flocks,*

*By shallow rivers to whose falls*

*Melodious birds sing madrigals.*

**Scheme used: Anaphora**—repeating words, phrases, or clauses at the beginning of successive sentences, clauses, or lines

In this poem, Christopher Marlowe wishes to impress upon his recipient all the glorious things they could do together, so it is fitting that he repeats "and we will." Also notice many of his suggestions for activities involve the "l" sound, which also begins the word "love." In this repetition Marlowe causes the reader to associate the suggested actions with love. Sneaky, sneaky, Marlowe!

# Drawing Practice

## Sonnet 18 ("Shall I compare thee to a summer's day?")
### by William Shakespeare (1609)

Shall I compare thee to a summer's day?

Thou art more lovely and more temperate:

Rough winds do shake the darling buds of

    May,

And summer's lease hath all too short a date:

Sometime too hot the eye of heaven shines,

And often is his gold complexion dimmed;

And every fair from fair sometime declines,

By chance or nature's changing course

    untrimmed;

But thy eternal summer shall not fade,

Nor lose possession of that fair thou ow'st;

*Nor shall death brag thou wander'st in his shade,*

*When in eternal lines to time thou grow'st:*

*So long as men can breathe or eyes can see,*

*So long lives this, and this gives life to thee.*

**Trope used: Simile**—**explicitly comparing two seemingly different things using "like" or "as"**

When a poet uses simile, he or she states an intent to draw a comparison, rather than allowing the reader to infer the comparison, as in a metaphor. In Sonnet 18 Shakespeare explores simile by stating that he will compare two different things (the woman he loves to a summer's day). Yet Shakespeare plays with the convention of simile—and of love poems—by going on to describe all the ways she transcends the comparison, and avoiding using the "like" or "as" that we expect to hear.

Poets often use simile because it sheds new light on each of the things being compared, leading the reader to rich new understandings. It also aids in describing the hard to describe—hence its common appearance in love letters.

Drawing Practice

## Sonnet 29 ("When, in disgrace with fortune and men's eyes") by William Shakespeare (1609)

When, in disgrace with Fortune and men's eyes,

I all alone beweep my outcast state,

And trouble deaf heaven with my bootless cries,

And look upon myself and curse my fate,

Wishing me like to one more rich in hope,

Featured like him, like him with friends
   possessed,

Desiring this man's art and that man's scope,

With what I most enjoy contented least;

Yet in these thoughts myself almost despising,

Haply I think on thee, and then my state,

Like to the lark at break of day arising

*From sullen earth sings hymns at heaven's gate;*

*For thy sweet love remembered such wealth brings*

*That then I scorn to change my state with kings.*

**Scheme used: Anadiplosis**—repeating the last word of one clause at the beginning of the next

Shakespeare, to no one's surprise, uses anadiplosis masterfully in this sonnet. In line 5 he says "Wishing me like to one more rich in hope." Then he uses the word "like" at the end of one phrase and the beginning of the next to emphasize his jealousy of other men:

> Featured like him, like him with friends possessed,
> Desiring this man's art and that man's scope,

He wants to be like this man, and like that man, desiring to be so many things. By repeating "like him" to mirror the following line, the reader gets a sense of how strong Shakespeare's desires are.

Drawing Practice

**DIVINE MEDITATION 10 ("BATTER MY HEART, THREE-PERSON'D GOD") BY JOHN DONNE (1635)**
*Numbering of the meditations, alternately called Holy Sonnets, varies from edition to edition. This number is consistent with the 1635 ordering.*

Batter my heart, three-person'd God, for you

As yet but knock, breathe, shine, and seek to

mend;

That I may rise and stand, o'erthrow me, and

bend

Your force to break, blow, burn, and make me

new.

I, like an usurped town to another due,

Labor to admit you, but O, to no end;

Reason, your viceroy in me, me should defend,

But is captived, and proves weak or untrue.

Yet dearly I love you, and would be loved fain,

*But am betrothed unto your enemy;*

*Divorce me, untie or break that knot again;*

*Take me to you, imprison me, for I,*

*Except you enthrall me, never shall be free,*

*Nor ever chaste, except you ravish me.*

**Scheme used: Anadiplosis**—repeating the last word of one clause at the beginning of the next

Towards the middle of this poem, Donne says, "Reason, your viceroy in me, me should defend," repeating "me" at the end of one clause and the beginning of the following clause. By adding the second "me," Donne breaks the line into smaller clauses, thereby fitting the rest of the poem, which Donne comprises of short consecutive clauses. He also emphasizes the subject's need for divine aid, since in this clause he talks about himself not as the subject, but as the direct object and the receiver.

Drawing Practice

# Divine Meditation 6 ("Death, be not proud, though some have called thee")
## by John Donne (1635)

Death, be not proud, though some have called thee
Mighty and dreadful, for thou art not so;
For those whom thou think'st thou dost overthrow
Die not, poor Death, nor yet canst thou kill me.
From rest and sleep, which but thy pictures be,
Much pleasure; then from thee much more must flow,
And soonest our best men with thee do go,
Rest of their bones, and soul's delivery.
Thou art slave to fate, chance, kings, and

*desperate men.*

*And dost with poison, war, and sickness dwell,*

*And poppy or charms can make us sleep as well*

*And better than thy stroke; why swell'st thou then?*

*One short sleep past, we wake eternally*

*And death shall be no more; Death, thou shalt die.*

**Trope used: Apostrophe**—speaking to an imaginary or absent person or an abstract quality

Poets have personified death for centuries (think of the Grim Reaper), but none with quite so much vehemence. John Donne clearly does not find death intimidating and determines to make that clear. How does he do this? First, he personifies death so he can talk to it. Then, he puts Death in his place by telling him not to be proud and continues to deride him through the entire poem, thereby comprising one of the most famous uses of apostrophe in all of literature.

**Nota Bene**: Modern editors have altered the punctuation slightly. The original first line read, "death be not proud," which could mean either that death is not proud, or he is telling death not to be proud. What do you think Donne meant?

Draw something that this poem makes you think of on your own paper, or move on to the next lesson.

### Excerpt from "Easter Wings" by George Herbert (1633)
*The Temple*

Lord, who createdst man in wealth and store,

Though foolishly he lost the same,

Decaying more and more

Till he became

Most poor:

With thee

O let me rise

As larks, harmoniously,

And sing this day thy victories:

Then shall the fall further the flight in me.

**Scheme used: Rhyme**—repeating the same consonant and vowel sound in the final emphasized syllable of a line

Herbert uses rhyme in a way we haven't seen before. Instead of making two consecutive lines rhyme with each other, he alternates rhyming lines like this: "store," "same," "more," "became." See how the rhyming words alternate? This adds interest and a sense of expectation in the reader because he or she knows how each line will end and is waiting for it.

**Nota Bene**: Look at the structure of the poem. Now turn it sideways. Do you see the shape of a bird's wings in the lines? Early editions of this poem printed the lines vertically to make the shape more apparent.

# Drawing Practice

## "Love (I)" by George Herbert (1633)
### The Temple

Immortal Love, author of this great frame,

   Sprung from that beauty which can never

     fade,

  How hath man parcel'd out Thy glorious name,

And thrown it on that dust which Thou hast

    made,

While mortal love doth all the title gain!

   Which siding with Invention, they together

  Bear all the sway, possessing heart and brain

(Thy workmanship) and give Thee share in

    neither.

Wit fancies beauty, beauty raiseth wit;

The world is theirs, they two play out the

game,

Thou standing by: and though Thy glorious

name

Wrought our deliverance from th' infernal pit,

Who sings Thy praise? Only a scarf or glove

Doth warm our hands, and make them write of

love.

**Scheme used: Antimetabole—repeating the same words in two successive clauses, but inverting the structure**

"Wit fancies beauty, beauty raiseth wit." By phrasing this in two parallel clauses, Herbert forces the reader to think about the difference between the two clauses, which here are the verbs "fancies" and "raiseth." It's also a playful turn of phrase, which is fitting, since the next line says "they two play out the game."

Draw something that this poem makes you think of on your own paper, or move on to the next lesson.

## "Redemption" by George Herbert (1633)
### The Temple

Having been tenant long to a rich lord,

Not thriving, I resolvèd to be bold,

And make a suit unto him, to afford

A new small-rented lease, and cancel th' old.

In heaven at his manor I him sought;

They told me there that he was lately gone

About some land, which he had dearly bought

Long since on earth, to take possession.

I straight returned, and knowing his great birth,

Sought him accordingly in great resorts—

In cities, theaters, gardens, parks, and courts;

> At length I heard a ragged noise and mirth
>
> Of thieves and murderers; there I him espied,
>
> Who straight, "Your suit is granted," said, and
>
> died.

**Scheme used: Anastrophe**—inverting the natural word order of a phrase, clause, or sentence

By changing the normal way of saying things, Herbert forces the reader to pay attention. This is prominent in the lines "In heaven at his manor I him sought" and "Of thieves and murderers; there I him espied." Typical syntax would be, "I sought him in heaven at his manor" and "I espied him there." Anastrophe allows Herbert to draw attention to the lines he wants to emphasize. In the first line he seeks his master in heaven, and in the second he finds him among sinners. This contrast is key to the poem.

Drawing Practice

**EXCERPT FROM "THE WORLD" BY HENRY VAUGHAN (1650)**
*SILEX SCINTILLANS*

I saw Eternity the other night,

Like a great ring of pure and endless light,

   All calm, as it was bright;

And round beneath it, Time in hours, days,

   years,

   Driv'n by the spheres

Like a vast shadow mov'd; in which the world

   And all her train were hurl'd.

The doting lover in his quaintest strain

   Did there complain;

Near him, his lute, his fancy, and his flights,

   Wit's sour delights.

*With gloves, and knots, the silly snares of*

*pleasure,*

*Yet his dear treasure*

*All scatter'd lay, while he his eyes did pour*

*Upon a flow'r.*

**Trope used: Simile**—explicitly comparing two seemingly different things using "like" or "as"

Imagine how epic it would be to see eternity! Afterward, of course, you would have to tell all your friends, so you would sit down to write about it. But how can you describe it? Vaughan learns from poets before him, such as Shakespeare and Homer, and turns to similes for help. In the second line he says eternity is "like a great ring of pure and endless light." Then he says in line 6, "Time…like a vast shadow mov'd." Vaughan creates a beautiful picture to help us understand eternity, wherein eternity is light, and time is its shadow. He takes two abstract ideas and made them visible.

Drawing Practice

**EXCERPT FROM BOOK I OF *PARADISE LOST* BY JOHN MILTON (1667)**

Of man's first disobedience, and the fruit

Of that forbidden tree, whose mortal taste

Brought death into the world, and all our woe,

With loss of Eden, till one greater Man

Restore us, and regain the blissful seat,

Sing, Heav'nly Muse, that on the secret top

Of Oreb, or of Sinai, didst inspire

That shepherd who first taught the chosen seed,

In the beginning how the heav'ns and earth

Rose out of Chaos: or if Sion hill

Delight thee more, and Siloa's brook that flowed

Fast by the oracle of God, I thence

Invoke thy aid to my advent'rous song,

That with no middle flight intends to soar

Above th' Aonian mount, while it pursues

Things unattempted yet in prose or rhyme.

And chiefly thou, O Spirit, that dost prefer

Before all temples th' upright heart and pure,

Instruct me, for thou know'st; thou from the first

Wast present, and, with mighty wings outspread,

Dove-like sat'st brooding on the vast Abyss

And mad'st it pregnant: what in me is dark

Illumine, what is low raise and support,

*That to the height of this great argument*

*I may assert Eternal Providence*

*And justify the ways of God to men.*

**Scheme used: Enjambment**—carrying the sense of one line of verse over to the next line without a pause

Milton adds auditory interest and variety, requiring the attention of the reader, by incorporating enjambment into his poetry. Were Milton to finish every thought at the end of each line, the poem would become mundane and stagnant, due to the length of this epic poem. Also, it allows the poem to be read more quickly and organically than if each line were to conclude a thought. The first three lines exemplify this technique, but note that the entire poem incorporates it.

# Drawing Practice

### "When I Consider How My Light Is Spent" by John Milton (1673)

When I consider how my light is spent,

Ere half my days, in this dark world and wide,

And that one talent which is death to hide

Lodged with me useless, though my soul more bent

To serve therewith my Maker, and present

My true account, lest he returning chide;

"Doth God exact day-labour, light denied?"

I fondly ask. But Patience, to prevent

That murmur, soon replies, "God doth not need

Either man's work or his own gifts; who best

*Bear his mild yoke, they serve him best. His state*

*Is kingly. Thousands at his bidding speed*

*And post o'er Land and Ocean without rest:*

*They also serve who only stand and wait."*

**Trope used: Metonymy**—referring to something by naming a closely related attribute or item

If you were to take this first line literally, Milton would wonder what objects absorb light, which probably wouldn't make sense in this poem. But Milton does not mean "light is spent" literally; rather he replaces days/years/life/time, etc. with the word "light," which multiplies his meaning in this opening line. He also gives an abstract idea (time) visible characteristics, making this line more potent.

**Nota Bene:** While metonymy and synecdoche seem very similar, they are not the same thing. Metonymy replaces a thing with a closely related attribute. Synecdoche uses part of something to represent the whole. For example, when T.S. Eliot writes, "I should have been a pair of ragged claws / Scuttling across the floors of silent seas," claws (the part) stand in for crabs (the whole).

Drawing Practice

# EXCERPTS FROM "CONTEMPLATIONS" BY ANNE BRADSTREET (1678)
## SEVERAL POEMS COMPILED WITH GREAT VARIETY OF WIT AND LEARNING

2. I wist not what to wish, yet sure thought I,

If so much excellence abide below,

How excellent is he that dwells on high?

Whose power and beauty by his works we know.

Sure he is goodness, wisdom, glory, light,

That hath this under world so richly dight.

More Heaven than Earth was here, no winter
 and no night

.................................................................

7. Art thou so full of glory that no Eye

Hath strength thy shining Rays once to behold?

And is thy splendid Throne erect so high?

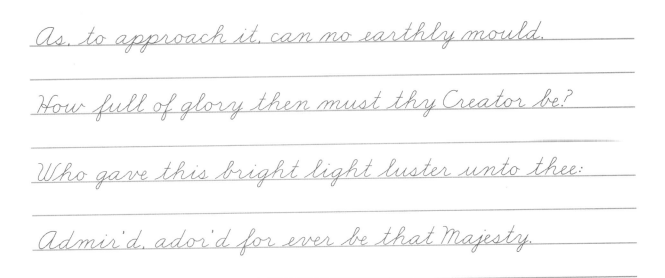

*As, to approach it, can no earthly mould.*

*How full of glory then must thy Creator be?*

*Who gave this bright light luster unto thee:*

*Admir'd, ador'd for ever be that Majesty.*

**Scheme used: Asyndeton**—omitting necessary conjunctions between clauses or words

Asyndeton, when used appropriately, adds power and intensity. In this poem, Anne Bradstreet frequently omits conjunctions, especially in line 5. There it forces the reader to place additional emphasis on each of the divine attributes—"goodness, wisdom, glory, light"—which she describes in the following line as "rich." This use of asyndeton, perhaps ironically, trips up the flow of thought and causes the reader to give equal weight to each attribute and a still greater weight to all of them together.

On a separate sheet of paper, copy the poem, and find a creative way (using color or images) to emphasize the glory, light, and richness of creation.

## Excerpt from "A Song for St. Cecilia's Day" by John Dryden (1687)

From harmony, from Heav'nly harmony

This universal frame began:

When Nature underneath a heap

Of jarring atoms lay,

And could not heave her head,

The tuneful voice was heard from high:

"Arise ye more than dead."

Then cold, and hot, and moist, and dry,

In order to their stations leap,

And Music's pow'r obey.

From harmony, from Heav'nly harmony

This universal frame began:

*From harmony to harmony*

*Through all the compass of the notes it ran,*

*The diapason closing full in man.*

**Trope used: Personification**—ascribing human characteristics to inanimate objects or abstract qualities

The poet imagines nature at the time of Genesis 1:1 as a woman trapped under a "heap / Of jarring atoms." Dryden composed this poem in honor of St. Cecilia, a Roman Christian woman who was martyred for her faith and whose legacy was often associated with music. In this poem, creation is an act of rescue. It is easier to imagine helping someone climb out of a pile of rubble than it is to imagine a state of nothingness. Dryden uses this trope to make the magnitude of creation understandable on a human level.

Drawing Practice

## Excerpt from "The Dying Christian to His Soul" by Alexander Pope (1712)

Hark! they whisper; angels say,

Sister Spirit, come away!

What is this absorbs me quite?

Steals my senses, shuts my sight,

Drowns my spirits, draws my breath?

Tell me, my soul, can this be death?

The world recedes; it disappears!

Heav'n opens on my eyes! my ears

With sounds seraphic ring!

Lend, lend your wings! I mount! I fly!

O Grave! where is thy victory?

O Death! where is thy sting?

## Scheme used: Parallelism—repeating the same grammatical order for a series of words, phrases, or clauses

Parallelism organizes ideas while creating rhythm and emphasis. Poets often use it to end a poem because of the sense of finality it creates, which makes it a brilliant scheme for Alexander Pope to use, since he's talking to Death. He's tying up his poem with no loose ends, while at the same time challenging death, the ultimate "end." In both the form (structure) and content (words) he says he does not fear death.

**Nota Bene:** Ancient Hebraic poetry, particularly Psalms and Proverbs, often uses parallelism to create emphasis. In Proverbs 11:19, "Righteousness brings one to life, evil brings one to death," the parallelism between the two clauses emphasizes the difference: righteousness and evil, life and death. Pope's closing lines certainly adopt Hebraic uses of parallelism, although he was not the first. Paul spoke them in 1 Corinthians 15:55.

Drawing Practice

**Excerpt from "On Virtue" by Phillis Wheatley (1773)**
*Poems on Various Subjects, Religious and Moral*

O thou bright jewel in my aim I strive

To comprehend thee. Thine own words declare

Wisdom is higher than a fool can reach.

I cease to wonder, and no more attempt

Thine height t'explore, or fathom thy profound.

But, O my soul, sink not into despair,

Virtue is near thee, and with gentle hand

Would now embrace thee, hovers o'er thine head.

Fain would the heaven-born soul with her

    converse,

Then seek, then court her for her promised bliss.

**Trope used: Apostrophe**—speaking to an imaginary or absent person or an abstract quality

When the poet speaks to Virtue ("O thou bright jewel") and her own soul ("O my soul") in this poem, she speaks to them as though they are characters standing before her, borrowing the Greek and Roman practice of personifying abstract qualities. This choice displays Wheatley's classical education; although she spent her childhood in slavery, she was permitted to read Milton, Virgil, and Homer alongside her owner's children.

## "The Tyger" by William Blake (1794)
### Songs of Experience

Tyger! Tyger! burning bright,

In the forests of the night,

What immortal hand or eye

Could frame thy fearful symmetry?

In what distant deeps or skies

Burnt the fire of thine eyes?

On what wings dare he aspire?

What the hand dare seize the fire?

And what shoulder, & what art,

Could twist the sinews of thy heart?

And when thy heart began to beat,

What dread hand? & what dread feet?

What the hammer? what the chain,

In what furnace was thy brain?

What the anvil? what dread grasp

Dare its deadly terrors clasp!

When the stars threw down their spears

And water'd heaven with their tears,

Did he smile his work to see?

Did he who made the Lamb make thee?

Tyger! Tyger! burning bright,

In the forests of the night,

*What immortal hand or eye,*

*Dare frame thy fearful symmetry?*

**Scheme used: Anaphora**—repeating words, phrases, or clauses at the beginning of successive sentences, clauses, or lines

What's the scheme William Blake used here? What could it be? Count how many times he said "what!" This poem includes many schemes, but we're going to focus on anaphora. The repetition of "what" increases the sense of wonderment and imagination Blake wants the reader to feel toward the tiger, and ultimately toward God. This repetition also draws attention to the places Blake omits it. Note the second to the last stanza where Blake asks, "Did he smile his work to see? Did he who made the Lamb make thee?" Before this stanza, Blake only wonders and imagines, but now he places the reader within time and place, asking a yes-or-no question. This reveals that these two questions are of utmost importance.

## Drawing Practice

**EXCERPT FROM "FROST AT MIDNIGHT" BY SAMUEL TAYLOR COLERIDGE (1798)**
collected in *SIBYLLINE LEAVES* (1817)

Therefore all seasons shall be sweet to thee,

Whether the summer clothe the general earth

With greenness, or the redbreast sit and sing

Betwixt the tufts of snow on the bare branch

Of mossy apple-tree, while the nigh thatch

Smokes in the sun-thaw; whether the

   eave-drops fall

Heard only in the trances of the blast,

Or if the secret ministry of frost

Shall hang them up in silent icicles,

Quietly shining to the quiet Moon.

**Scheme used: Alliteration**—repeating consonant sounds, often at the beginning of words

Coleridge incorporates the scheme of alliteration in the first line of "Frost at Midnight" by repeating the sibilant "s" sound at the beginning of multiple words. When you hear "seasons shall be sweet," which seasons come to mind? Probably summer and spring, not only because of their sweetness, but because they too begin with an "s." Herein lies the power of alliteration: the author can create unspoken comparisons. So even before you go on to read of summer in the next line, Coleridge has brought spring and summer to your mind.

**Nota Bene:** Poets of old often did this with poems about heroes and villains. They included positive adjectives with the same first sound as the hero, and negative adjectives with the same first sound as the villain. Think of the vile villain Voldemort: is it a coincidence his name begins with a "V?" I think not.

Drawing Practice

# "My Heart Leaps Up" by William Wordsworth (1802)
## *Poems, in Two Volumes* (1807)

My heart leaps up when I behold

  A rainbow in the sky:

So was it when my life began;

So is it now I am a man;

So be it when I shall grow old,

  Or let me die!

The Child is father of the Man;

And I could wish my days to be

Bound each to each by natural piety.

**Scheme used: Anaphora**—repeating words, phrases, or clauses at the beginning of successive sentences, clauses, or lines

Wordsworth repeats the word "So" at the beginning of three successive lines. Each one describes a phase of life: infancy, adulthood, and old age. Using the same word ties each of those three clauses back to the first clause, "My heart leaps up when I behold / A rainbow in the sky." Wordsworth uses this technique to show that the speaker has consistently experienced and will continue to experience the wonder of a rainbow, no matter how old he gets.

## Drawing Practice

## Excerpts from "Defence of Fort McHenry" by Francis Scott Key (c. 1814)
*Words Aptly Spoken: American Documents*

O say can you see, by the dawn's early light,

What so proudly we hail'd at the twilight's last gleaming,

Whose broad stripes and bright stars, thro' the perilous fight,

O'er the ramparts we watch'd, were so gallantly streaming?

And the rockets' red glare, the bombs bursting in air,

Gave proof thro' the night that our flag was still there.

O say, does that star-spangled banner yet wave

O'er the land of the free and the home of the brave?

O thus be it ever when free-men shall stand
Between their lov'd home and the war's desolation;
Blest with vict'ry and peace, may the heav'n-rescued land
Praise the Pow'r that hath made and preserv'd us a nation!
Then conquer we must, when our cause it is just,
And this be our motto: "In God is our trust."

*And the star-spangled banner in triumph shall wave*

*O'er the land of the free and the home of the brave!*

**Scheme used: Enjambment**—carrying the sense of one line over to the next line of verse without a pause

Francis Scott Key uses enjambment much like Milton does in *Paradise Lost* to add interest and variety to his poem. Key, however, mixes enjambment with short, complete lines rather than relying on enjambment alone. Notice how the poem begins with many short clauses, each about half a line. If you read it aloud you can really hear the breaks. Then, he adds an enjambed line such as, "Whose broad stripes and bright stars, thro' the perilous fight / O'er the ramparts we watch'd, were so gallantly streaming?" This long line creates anticipation, as the reader must wait for the verb "were streaming" to find out what happened to the broad stripes and bright stars of the American flag.

## Drawing Practice

## "OZYMANDIAS" BY PERCY BYSSHE SHELLEY (1818)
### Published in *The Examiner*, January 11, 1818

I met a traveller from an antique land,

Who said—"Two vast and trunkless legs of stone

Stand in the desert. ...Near them, on the sand,

Half sunk a shattered visage lies, whose frown,

And wrinkled lip, and sneer of cold command,

Tell that its sculptor well those passions read

Which yet survive, stamped on these lifeless things,

The hand that mocked them, and the heart that fed;

And on the pedestal, these words appear:

My name is Ozymandias, King of Kings;

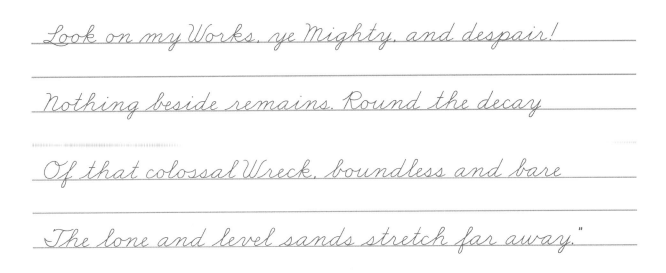

**Trope used: Irony**—saying one thing but implying the opposite

In this poem Shelley describes the ruins of an old statue of King Ozymandias, which is engraved with the words, "Look on my Works, ye Mighty, and despair!" Is Shelley telling the reader to despair at the mighty works of this king? Hopefully you find that rather silly, since "nothing beside remains." Rather, he includes these words ironically, to mean the exact opposite without having to bluntly state it. Irony often makes it possible to subtly say something without actually saying it.

Drawing Practice

**EXCERPT FROM "TO A WATERFOWL" BY WILLIAM CULLEN BRYANT (1815)**
*POEMS* (1821)

There is a Power whose care

Teaches thy way along that pathless coast,—

The desert and illimitable air,—

Lone wandering, but not lost.

All day thy wings have fanned

At that far height, the cold thin atmosphere:

Yet stoop not, weary, to the welcome land,

Though the dark night is near.

And soon that toil shall end,

Soon shalt thou find a summer home, and rest,

And scream among thy fellows; reeds shall

bend

Soon, o'er thy sheltered nest.

Thou'rt gone, the abyss of heaven

Hath swallowed up thy form; yet, on my heart

Deeply hath sunk the lesson thou hast given,

And shall not soon depart.

He, who, from zone to zone,

Guides through the boundless sky thy certain

flight,

In the long way that I must tread alone,

Will lead my steps aright.

**Trope used: Personification**—ascribing human characteristics to inanimate objects or abstract qualities

William Cullen Bryant carries the reader on this flight alongside the bird throughout the first three stanzas, promising rest in the third stanza. Then, shockingly, he says, "Thou'rt gone, the abyss of heaven hath swallowed up thy form." By personifying heaven as having swallowed up the bird's form, Bryant makes this death even more powerful and vivid, one of the greatest strengths of personification.

**Nota Bene:** Once again we see a poet personifying an aspect of death.

# Drawing Practice

**EXCERPT FROM "ODE ON A GRECIAN URN" BY JOHN KEATS (1819)**

O Attic shape! Fair attitude! with brede

    Of marble men and maidens overwrought,

With forest branches and the trodden weed;

    Thou, silent form, dost tease us out of

thought

As doth eternity: Cold Pastoral!

    When old age shall this generation waste,

    Thou shalt remain, in midst of other

woe

Than ours, a friend to man, to whom thou

say'st,

    "Beauty is truth, truth beauty,—that is all

*Ye know on earth, and all ye need to know."*

**Trope used: Ekphrasis**—describing a work of visual art in words

Every ancient Roman boy who attended school studied ekphrasis until he mastered it. Primarily because it's a powerful aid in memorization, developing the imagination, and building an appreciation for the arts, which were of course of utmost importance to the Romans. Remember the lengthy description of Achilles' shield in *The Iliad* or the detailed descriptions of the murals in Dido's palace in *The Aeneid*? These famous uses of ekphrasis reveal how it can make the reader feel present in the scene, rather than just intellectually understanding the story. The ancient poets also used ekphrasis to give honor to the artist and art being described—the greater the description, the more honor bestowed. It is fitting for Keats to praise a Grecian urn using this ancient technique.

**Nota Bene:** This poem is a scheme and trope treasure trove! What other ones do you see?

Drawing Practice

## "The Floweret" by Alexander Pushkin (1828)
*Poems by Alexander Pushkin*, Translated by Ivan Panin (1888)

A floweret, withered, odorless

In a book forgot I find;

And already strange reflection

Cometh into my mind.

Bloomed, where? when? in what spring?

And how long ago? And plucked by whom?

Was it by a strange hand? Was it by a dear hand?

And wherefore left thus here?

Was it in memory of a tender meeting?

Was it in memory of a fated parting?

Was it in memory of a lonely walk?

In the peaceful fields or in the shady woods?

Lives he still? Lives she still?

And where their nook this very day?

Or are they too withered

Like unto this unknown floweret?

**Scheme used: Alliosis**—presenting alternatives in parallel form

In this poem, Pushkin's narrator exercises his imagination as he tries to determine the origin of a dried flower. You can almost hear the "either/or" as he considers various possibilities. Specifically, in the second stanza, he ponders whether the person who picked the flower was known or unknown to the person who placed it in the book. In the third stanza, he weighs three possible alternatives: meeting, walk, and parting. In this poem, Pushkin uses questions adeptly to show his readers how many stories a simple object can contain.

Drawing Practice

## "Liberty for All" by William Lloyd Garrison (1831)
### Published in *The Liberator*
#### Words Aptly Spoken: American Documents

They tell me, Liberty! that in thy name

I may not plead for all the human race;

That some are born to bondage and disgrace,

Some to a heritage of woe and shame,

And some to power supreme, and glorious fame:

With my whole soul I spurn the doctrine base,

And, as an equal brotherhood, embrace

All people, and for all fair freedom claim!

Know this, O man! whate'er thy earthly fate—

God never made a tyrant nor a slave:

Woe, then, to those who dare to desecrate

His glorious image!—for to all He gave

*Eternal rights, which none may violate;*

*And, by a mighty hand, the oppressed He yet*

*shall save!*

**Scheme used: Parallelism**—repeating the same grammatical order for a series of words, phrases, or clauses

In lines three, four, and five above, Garrison repeats the same grammatical structure "some to ____ and _____" three times, each with contrasting content. The first of the three lines speaks of slavery, the most degrading state of humanity. He then rises to people born "to a heritage of woe and shame," and then to the powerful and glorious, ascending in power as the lines in the poem ascend. This hierarchical construction sets up the next few lines, where Garrison says he spurns this doctrine, and that all men are equal.

Drawing Practice

## Excerpt from part I of "The Rime of the Ancient Mariner" by Samuel Taylor Coleridge (1797)

"And a good south wind sprung up behind;

The Albatross did follow,

And every day, for food or play,

Came to the mariners' hollo!

In mist or cloud, on mast or shroud,

It perched for vespers nine;

Whiles all the night, through fog-smoke white,

Glimmered the white moon-shine."

"God save thee, ancient Mariner!

From the fiends, that plague thee thus!—

Why look'st thou so?"—With my cross-bow

*I shot the Albatross.*

**Scheme used: Consonance**—repeating consonant sounds in adjacent words with different vowel sounds

With a wingspan like a modern-day dinosaur, the albatross is indubitably one of the most epic birds alive, so it's fitting that Samuel Taylor Coleridge includes it in his epic narrative poem. Throughout the poem, Coleridge repeats the "s" sound, building to the most important instance of consonance which occurs in the last line: "I shot the albatross." The structure of this line is almost chiastic, too, with "t" sounds sandwiched between "s" sounds. The repetition of "s" sounds throughout these stanzas allows Coleridge to give more weight to the final mention of the albatross, making it even more, well...epic.

Drawing Practice

**EXCERPT FROM "A PSALM OF LIFE" BY HENRY WADSWORTH LONGFELLOW (1838)**
*VOICES OF THE NIGHT* (1839)

Lives of great men all remind us

We can make our lives sublime,

And, departing, leave behind us

Footsteps on the sands of time;

Footsteps, that perhaps another,

Sailing o'er life's solemn main,

A forlorn and shipwrecked brother,

Seeing, shall take heart again.

Let us then be up and doing,

With a heart for any fate;

Still achieving, still pursuing,

*Learn to labor and to wait.*

**Trope used: Metonymy**—referring to something by naming a closely related attribute or item

In the line "seeing, shall take heart again," Longfellow does not suggest they take up a real bloody heart once more, nor did you think he meant this. You knew that when he said "heart" he meant courage, and in the next line when he again says "heart" he really means love or acceptance. By using "heart" twice within two lines, Longfellow adds to the rhyme scheme and builds emphasis. He also creates a parallel between the forlorn sailor and the "us" he speaks to in the following stanza.

## Excerpt from "Ulysses" by Alfred, Lord Tennyson (1833)
### Poems, in Two Volumes (1842)

There lies the port; the vessel puffs her sail:

There gloom the dark, broad seas. My mariners,

Souls that have toiled, and wrought, and

   thought with me—

That ever with a frolic welcome took

The thunder and the sunshine, and opposed

Free hearts, free foreheads—you and I are old;

Old age hath yet his honour and his toil.

Death closes all: but something ere the end,

Some work of noble note, may yet be done,

Not unbecoming men that strove with Gods.

The lights begin to twinkle from the rocks:

The long day wanes: the slow moon climbs: the deep

Moans round with many voices. Come, my friends,

'Tis not too late to seek a newer world.

Push off, and sitting well in order smite

The sounding furrows; for my purpose holds

To sail beyond the sunset, and the baths

Of all the western stars, until I die.

It may be that the gulfs will wash us down:

It may be we shall touch the Happy Isles,

And see the great Achilles, whom we knew.

*Though much is taken, much abides; and though*

*We are not now that strength which in old days*

*Moved earth and heaven, that which we are, we*

*are—*

*One equal temper of heroic hearts,*

*Made weak by time and fate, but strong in will*

*To strive, to seek, to find, and not to yield.*

**Scheme used: Antithesis**—arranging contrasting ideas in adjacent clauses, often in the same grammatical pattern

Tennyson masterfully utilizes repetition, for he always repeats with intention. The idea that the sailors might either drown or reach the "Happy Isles" is in itself dramatic and emotional, but when combined with the repetition of parallel structure, Tennyson amplifies the emotion. He pulls the reader into the emotional turbulence of the moment, where great happiness or great misfortune may occur.

## Drawing Practice

**EXCERPT FROM "THE RAVEN" BY EDGAR ALLAN POE (1845)**
**Published in *The American Review*, February 1845**

Much I marvelled this ungainly fowl to

hear discourse so plainly,

Though its answer little meaning—little

relevancy bore;

For we cannot help agreeing that no

sublunary being

Ever yet was blessed with seeing bird above

his chamber door—

Bird or beast upon the sculptured bust above

his chamber door,

With such name as "Nevermore."

But the raven, sitting lonely on the placid

bust, spoke only

That one word, as if his soul in that one word

he did outpour.

Nothing farther then he uttered—not a feather

then he fluttered—

Till I scarcely more than muttered "Other

friends have flown before—

On the morrow he will leave me, as my hopes

have flown before."

Quoth the raven, "Nevermore."

**Scheme used: Epistrophe**—repeating words, phrases, or clauses at the end of successive sentences, clauses, or lines

Epistrophe comes from the Greek meaning "turning about" or "upon turning." Like anaphora, it has a strong ability to create mood, rhythm, and emphasis. However, because epistrophe places emphasis at the end of each clause, it can be more dramatic.

In "The Raven," Poe repeats "above his chamber door" at the end of the first stanza of this excerpt, leading us to expect he will say it a third time. However, he interrupts his own epistrophe by saying "nevermore" at the end of the sentence. He ends the second stanza with same incomplete epistrophe and interruption. This impresses upon the reader the feeling of the subject as he hears "nevermore," while also communicating the finality of the raven's pronunciation.

## Drawing Practice

**"High waving heather, 'neath stormy blasts bending" by Emily Brontë (1836)**
*Poems by Currer, Ellis, and Acton Bell (1846)*

High waving heather, 'neath stormy blasts bending,

Midnight and moonlight and bright shining stars;

Darkness and glory rejoicingly blending,

Earth rising to heaven and heaven descending,

Man's spirit away from its drear dongeon sending,

Bursting the fetters and breaking the bars.

All down the mountain sides, wild forest lending

One mighty voice to the life-giving wind;

Rivers their banks in the jubilee rending.

Fast through the valleys a reckless course wending.

Wider and deeper their waters extending.

Leaving a desolate desert behind.

Shining and lowering and swelling and dying.

Changing for ever from midnight to noon;

Roaring like thunder, like soft music sighing.

Shadows on shadows advancing and flying.

Lightning-bright flashes the deep gloom defying.

Coming as swiftly and fading as soon.

**Scheme used: Rhyme**—repeating the same consonant and vowel sound in the final emphasized syllable of a line

This poem also ought to be read aloud, in part because of Emily Brontë's splendid use of rhyme and meter. The rhyme scheme for each stanza in this poem is ABAAAB. Because four of the six lines have the same final syllable—Brontë loves to use present participles!—the poem seems to gallop along the page, the same way that the wind and the river and the lightning gallop down the mountain-sides, and also the same way, Brontë suggests, that a man's soul lunges toward freedom.

Drawing Practice

**Sonnet 43 ("How do I love thee? Let me count the ways")**
by Elizabeth Barrett Browning (1850)
*Sonnets from the Portuguese*

How do I love thee? Let me count the ways.

I love thee to the depth and breadth and height

My soul can reach, when feeling out of sight

For the ends of Being and ideal Grace.

I love thee to the level of every day's

Most quiet need, by sun and candlelight.

I love thee freely, as men strive for Right;

I love thee purely, as they turn from Praise.

I love thee with the passion put to use

In my old griefs, and with my childhood's

    faith.

I love thee with a love I seemed to lose

*With my lost saints—I love thee with the breath,*

*Smiles, tears, of all my life!—and, if God choose,*

*I shall but love thee better after death.*

**Scheme used: Anaphora**—repeating words, phrases, or clauses at the beginning of successive sentences, clauses, or lines

Elizabeth Browning uses anaphora here for rhythm and emphasis. She clearly didn't want to leave any room for doubt (perhaps the one she loved was bad at reading between the lines!).

Just like other uses of anaphora we have seen, the repetition draws attention to the difference. Twice Browning alters the phrase "I love thee." Can you find them? They are in the first and last lines: "How do I love thee" and "I shall but love thee better." When the reader hears the last line, even before any mention of death, they hear the phrase "I love thee" broken by the two foreign words "shall but." By changing the structure of this last line, Browning echoes the meaning of the poem, in which earthly love grows when it meets eternity.

Drawing Practice

**EXCERPT FROM "NATHAN HALE" BY FRANCIS M. FINCH (1853)**
**PRESENTED AT THE CENTENARY OF THE LINONIAN SOCIETY AT YALE**
*WORDS APTLY SPOKEN: AMERICAN DOCUMENTS*

'Neath the blue morn, the sunny morn,

He dies upon the tree;

And he mourns that he can lose

But one life for Liberty;

And in the blue morn, the sunny morn,

His spirit-wings are free.

But his last words, his message-words,

They burn, lest friendly eye

Should read how proud and calm

A patriot could die,

With his last words, his dying words,

A soldier's battle-cry.

**Scheme used: Repotia**—repeating a phrase with some variation of style, word choice, or tone

Based on the first line of the poem alone, what would you expect the mood of the poem to be? A "blue" and "sunny" morning conjures up a sense of happiness, so that the next line comes as even more of a shock: "He dies upon the tree." When the phrase "the blue morn, the sunny morn" is repeated a second time, it carries a much heavier mood. This use of repotia—repeating the same line with different moods—allows Finch to imply that joy, sacrifice, and liberty are closely related.

Drawing Practice

**EXCERPTS FROM "CHARGE OF THE LIGHT BRIGADE"**
BY ALFRED, LORD TENNYSON (1854)
PUBLISHED IN *THE EXAMINER*, DECEMBER 9, 1854

*II*

"Forward, the Light Brigade!"

Was there a man dismayed?

Not though the soldier knew

   Someone had blundered.

Theirs not to make reply,

Theirs not to reason why,

Theirs but to do and die.

Into the valley of Death

   Rode the six hundred.

V

Cannon to right of them,

Cannon to left of them,

Cannon behind them

   Volleyed and thundered;

Stormed at with shot and shell,

While horse and hero fell.

They that had fought so well

Came through the jaws of Death,

Back from the mouth of hell,

All that was left of them,

   Left of six hundred.

**Scheme used: Anaphora**—repeating words, phrases, or clauses at the beginning of successive sentences, clauses, or lines

Tennyson begins the poem in what seems to be a pretty routine rhyming pattern. After we hear the first two lines end in "brigade" and "dismayed," it seems he will continue with an AABB structure. So on the fourth line we expect him to rhyme with "knew" from the previous line, but instead he throws off the structure altogether! All of a sudden we hear "someone had blundered." Then Tennyson changes the structure of the poem even more with the use of anaphora, repeating "theirs" at the beginning of three consecutive lines. The combination of rhyme and anaphora fixes the reader's attention on that fatal blunder.

Drawing Practice

**Excerpt from Part I of "The Song of Hiawatha" by Henry Wadsworth Longfellow (1855)**
*Words Aptly Spoken: American Literature*

From the river came the warriors,

Clean and washed from all their war-paint;

On the banks their clubs they buried,

Buried all their warlike weapons.

Gitche Manito, the mighty,

The Great Spirit, the creator,

Smiled upon his helpless children!

And in silence all the warriors

Broke the red stone of the quarry,

Smoothed and formed it into Peace-Pipes...

**Scheme used: Anadiplosis**—repeating the last word of one clause at the beginning of the next

This is an excerpt from a longer poem about the American Indian god Gitche Manito, who tells his warriors to live in peace with each other. To do this, they symbolically bury their weapons, letting violence and strife die, and live a new kind of life. Longfellow uses anadiplosis, repeating the word "buried" back-to-back in the third and fourth lines, to emphasize the importance of the burial of their weapons and the rebirth of the warriors to a new life of peace.

# Drawing Practice

## "A Better Resurrection" by Christina Rossetti (1862)
*Goblin Market and Other Poems*

I have no wit, no words, no tears;
   My heart within me like a stone
Is numbed too much for hopes or fears;
   Look right, look left, I dwell alone;
I lift mine eyes, but dimm'd with grief
   No everlasting hills I see;
My life is in the falling leaf:
   O Jesus, quicken me.

My life is like a faded leaf,
   My harvest dwindled to a husk;
Truly my life is void and brief
   And tedious in the barren dusk;

My life is like a frozen thing.

No bud nor greenness can I see:

Yet rise it shall—the sap of Spring;

O Jesus, rise in me.

My life is like a broken bowl,

A broken bowl that cannot hold

One drop of water for my soul

Or cordial in the searching cold;

Cast in the fire the perished thing;

Melt and remould it, till it be

A royal cup for Him my King:

O Jesus, drink of me.

**Trope used: Simile**—explicitly comparing two seemingly different things using "like" or "as"

Consider the lines, "my life is like a faded leaf, my harvest dwindled to a husk: truly my life is void and brief." What does this image make you think of? Can you imagine feeling a faded leaf in your hands? Perhaps it crumbles, or maybe it feels cold and dry. This imagery is powerful because we have all encountered a faded leaf and know that it means the end of summer and beginning of winter. So when the poet compares her life to this kind of leaf, we have a more emotional and vivid response than if she had simply said her life was "void and brief." By combining many similes like this one, Rossetti paints a complete picture of her life, making us feel that we know her.

# Drawing Practice

### Excerpt from "Paul Revere's Ride" by Henry Wadsworth Longfellow (1861)
*Words Aptly Spoken: American Documents*

Listen, my children, and you shall hear

Of the midnight ride of Paul Revere,

On the eighteenth of April, in Seventy-five;

Hardly a man is now alive

Who remembers that famous day and year.

He said to his friend, "If the British march

By land or sea from the town to-night,

Hang a lantern aloft in the belfry arch

Of the North Church tower as a signal light,—

One, if by land, and two, if by sea;

And I on the opposite shore will be,

Ready to ride and spread the alarm

*Through every Middlesex village and farm.*

*For the country-folk to be up and to arm."*

**Scheme used: Anastrophe**—inverting the natural word order of a phrase, clause, or sentence

Longfellow changes the normal syntax several times in this excerpt. For example, he writes, "And I on the opposite shore will be." Natural word order would be, "I will be on the opposite shore." Anastrophe adds interest and beauty, but it also enables other devices such as rhyme. Longfellow changes the syntax to allow "be" to rhyme with "sea."

Drawing Practice

**Excerpt from *The Wagoner of the Alleghanies* by Thomas B. Read (1863)**
*Words Aptly Spoken: American Documents*

Such was the winter's awful sight

For many a dreary day and night,

What time our country's hope forlorn,

Of every needed comfort shorn,

Lay housed within a hurried tent,

Where every keen blast found a rent,

And oft the snow was seen to sift

Along the floor its piling drift,

Or, mocking the scant blanket's fold,

Across the night-couch frequent rolled;

Where every path by a soldier beat,

Or every track where a sentinel stood.

Still held the print of naked feet.

And oft the crimson stains of blood;

..................................................

Such was the winter that prevailed

Within the crowded, frozen gorge;

Such were the horrors that assailed

The patriot band at Valley Forge.

It was a midnight storm of woes

To clear the sky for Freedom's morn;

And such must ever be the throes

The hour when Liberty is born.

**Scheme used: Parallelism**—repeating the same grammatical order for a series of words, phrases, or clauses

"Such was the winter's awful sight," "Such was the winter that prevailed," "Such were the horrors that assailed, "And such must ever be the throes": these lines share the same grammatical structure, thereby paralleling each other. Thomas Read repeats this structure to two ends, the first, to create a rhythm and flow, the second, to emphasize the truth of his account. He ensures that the reader understands these horrors actually happened, and happened out of necessity.

## Drawing Practice

### Excerpt from "O Captain! My Captain!" By Walt Whitman (1865)
*Sequel to Drum-Taps (1865)*

O Captain! my Captain! our fearful trip is done,

The ship has weather'd every rack, the prize

we sought is won,

The port is near, the bells I hear, the people all

exulting,

While follow eyes the steady keel, the vessel

grim and daring;

But O heart! heart! heart!

O the bleeding drops of red,

Where on the deck my Captain lies,

Fallen cold and dead.

**Scheme used: Epizeuxis**—repeating a word or phrase emphatically for effect

In the first four stanzas, Walt Whitman writes in short continuous clauses, as one would do when very excited. But then, in the midst of this excitement, he inserts "heart! heart! heart!" which alters the rhythm and tone of the whole poem. It acts as a break, which allows Whitman to transition into the despair of the following lines. Poets often use epizeuxis in this manner, allowing a change in the rhythm, sound, or tone.

Drawing Practice

### EXCERPT FROM "DOVER BEACH" BY MATTHEW ARNOLD (1867)

The sea is calm tonight.

The tide is full, the moon lies fair

Upon the straits—on the French coast the light

Gleams and is gone; the cliffs of England stand,

Glimmering and vast, out in the tranquil bay.

Come to the window, sweet is the night air!

Only, from the long line of spray

Where the sea meets the moon-blanched land,

Listen! you hear the grating roar

Of pebbles which the waves draw back, and
 fling,

At their return, up the high strand,

*Begin, and cease, and then again begin,*

*With tremulous cadence slow, and bring*

*The eternal note of sadness in.*

**Scheme used: Epanalepsis**—repeating a word or words at the beginning and end of a phrase or clause (broadly--a refrain)

Poets can use epanalepsis in many different ways by varying the distance between the repeated words. In this instance, Arnold repeats "begin" at the beginning and end of a line. Later, you will see epanalesis where the repeated words are further and further apart.

One way that epanalepsis can be used is similar to the way that you may have written your papers—by putting the thesis at the beginning and the end of the essay. This ensures that the reader knows clearly what the point is all the way through. With that in mind, read the last five lines of this excerpt above. Notice how he uses the repetition of "begin" to describe the eternal cadence of the waves? Instead of simply saying the waves never stop, he repeats "begin" to mirror the action of waves and ensure that the reader understands the eternal nature of the waves, always beginning again.

Drawing Practice

## "Pied Beauty" by Gerard Manley Hopkins (1877)

Glory be to God for dappled things—

For skies of couple-colour as a brinded cow;

    For rose-moles all in stipple upon trout that swim;

Fresh-firecoal chestnut-falls; finches' wings;

    Landscape plotted and pieced—fold, fallow, and plough;

    And all trades, their gear and tackle and trim.

All things counter, original, spare, strange;

    Whatever is fickle, freckled (who knows how?)

    With swift, slow; sweet, sour; adazzle, dim;

*He fathers-forth whose beauty is past change:*

*Praise him.*

**Trope used: Congeries**—accumulating different words to create an overall emotional effect

While the items listed in this poem are, on the surface, seemingly disconnected and contradictory, Hopkins chose them intentionally to build a coherent whole. This scheme works similar to climax by building words one upon the other to create one common picture. In this case, all the listed things lead to amazement at the glory of God, and an offering of praise.

**Nota Bene:** Congeries is sometimes defined as a figure of amplification or a scheme, as well as a trope.

Drawing Practice

## "The Tide Rises, The Tide Falls" by Henry Wadsworth Longfellow (1879)
### Poetical Works (1890)

The tide rises, the tide falls,

The twilight darkens, the curlew calls;

Along the sea-sands damp and brown

The traveller hastens toward the town,

   And the tide rises, the tide falls.

Darkness settles on roofs and walls,

But the sea, the sea in the darkness calls;

The little waves, with their soft, white hands,

Efface the footprints in the sands,

   And the tide rises, the tide falls.

The morning breaks; the steeds in their stalls

*Stamp and neigh, as the hostler calls;*

*The day returns, but nevermore*

*Returns the traveller to the shore,*

*And the tide rises, the tide falls.*

**Scheme used: Epanalepsis**—repeating a word or words at the beginning and end of a phrase or clause (broadly--a refrain)

As you may have noticed, poets often use epanalepsis when describing waves, because its form mirrors the repetition of the waves. In this instance, Longfellow repeats the phrase "the tide rises, the tide falls" to contrast the regularity of the tides with the changes occurring in the rest of the world, particularly for the traveler. As the tide rises and falls, the footprints are washed away, the sun rises, and the traveler leaves never to return, and still the tide rises and falls in a constant rhythm.

Drawing Practice

## "The New Colossus" by Emma Lazarus (1883)
*Words Aptly Spoken: American Documents*

Not like the brazen giant of Greek fame

With conquering limbs astride from land to
 land;

Here at our sea-washed, sunset gates shall stand

A mighty woman with a torch, whose flame

Is the imprisoned lightning, and her name

Mother of Exiles. From her beacon-hand

Glows world-wide welcome; her mild eyes
 command

The air-bridged harbor that twin cities frame.

"Keep, ancient lands, your storied pomp!" cries she

With silent lips. "Give me your tired, your poor,

*Your huddled masses yearning to breathe free.*

*The wretched refuse of your teeming shore.*

*Send these, the homeless, tempest-tossed to me,*

*I lift my lamp beside the golden door!"*

**Scheme used: Chiasmus**—repeating ideas but inverting the grammatical structure

This structure can be complicated. It comes from the Greek letter *chi*, which looks like an "x." In the first line, Lazarus mentions a giant statue, the Colossus of Rhodes, and then describes where and how it stands ("with conquering limbs astride from land to land"). In the third and fourth lines, she describes America's "sea-washed sunset gates" first, and then describes the giant who stands there, the Statue of Liberty. So, the structure of these lines goes like this: giant statue (A), standing (B); standing (B), giant statue (A). This is a chiastic structure. If A and B were written like mathematical fractions (A/B and B/A), you could draw a line from one "B" to the other "B" and from "A" to "A" to create an "x" shape.

Drawing Practice

## "Crossing the Bar" by Alfred, Lord Tennyson (1889)
### *Demeter and Other Poems*

Sunset and evening star,
 And one clear call for me!
And may there be no moaning of the bar,
 When I put out to sea,

But such a tide as moving seems asleep,
 Too full for sound and foam,
When that which drew from out the boundless deep
 Turns again home.

Twilight and evening bell,
 And after that the dark!

And may there be no sadness of farewell,

When I embark;

For though from out our bourne of Time and

Place

The flood may bear me far,

I hope to see my Pilot face to face

When I have crossed the bar.

**Trope used: Metaphor**—**implicitly comparing two seemingly different things**

Have you ever gone swimming in the ocean, and reached a place you think too deep to stand, but then you find a sand bar and you discover you can easily stand? In this poem, Tennyson draws a metaphor between that bar and death. It's the last spot of rest before you cross over into the deep.

**Nota Bene:** Death itself is often talked about in poetry using metaphor, simile, or personification. If you think about it, this makes sense—no one living has ever experienced it!

Draw something that this poem makes you think of on your own paper, or move on to the next lesson.

## "The Lake Isle of Innisfree" by William Butler Yeats (1890)

I will arise and go now, and go to Innisfree,

And a small cabin build there, of clay and
   wattles made;

Nine bean-rows will I have there, a hive for
   the honey-bee,

And live alone in the bee-loud glade.

And I shall have some peace there, for peace
   comes dropping slow,

Dropping from the veils of the morning to
   where the cricket sings;

There midnight's all a glimmer, and noon a
   purple glow,

*And evening full of the linnet's wings.*

*I will arise and go now, for always night and day*

*I hear lake water lapping with low sounds by the shore;*

*While I stand on the roadway, or on the pavements grey,*

*I hear it in the deep heart's core.*

**Trope used: Onomatopoeia**—using words whose sound echoes the sense of the word

You have to read at least that last stanza aloud to really enjoy it fully. Tell me you don't hear "lake water lapping with low sounds" in your deep heart's core, and I will say you must not have a deep heart's core! I would like to attribute this sound to magic, but in reality Yeats achieved this by repeating the "l" rhythmically throughout the line, replicating the sound of water lapping.

Draw something that this poem makes you think of on your own paper, or move on to the next lesson.

**EXCERPT FROM "TO AN ATHLETE DYING YOUNG" BY A.E. HOUSMAN (1896)**
*A SHROPSHIRE LAD*

The time you won your town the race

We chaired you through the market-place;

Man and boy stood cheering by,

And home we brought you shoulder-high.

Today, the road all runners come,

Shoulder-high we bring you home,

And set you at your threshold down,

Townsman of a stiller town.

Smart lad, to slip betimes away

From fields where glory does not stay,

And early though the laurel grows

*It withers quicker than the rose.*

**Trope used: Metaphor**—implicitly comparing two seemingly different things

Housman draws a metaphor upon the life of a runner. He begins by remembering real-life events, when the runner won the race, when they celebrated him, and when they brought him home. In the next stanzas, he uses those same events as metaphors to describe the runner's death. They bring him home, carrying his body, on the road all runners come, which symbolizes death. And still they celebrate him, who, like the laurels that winners wear, withered and died in his prime.

**Nota Bene:** This is a metaphor rather than a simile because Housman does not use "like" or "as" to draw the comparison. He chooses to use metaphor instead to decrease the divide between the metaphorical and the literal. Perhaps he does so to decrease the divide between life and death.

Drawing Practice

**EXCERPT FROM "DEFENSE OF THE ALAMO" BY JOAQUIN MILLER (1898)**
*POEMS OF AMERICAN PATRIOTISM 1776–1898*
*WORDS APTLY SPOKEN: AMERICAN DOCUMENTS*

All day—all day and all night; and the

morning? so slow,

Through the battle smoke mantling the Alamo.

Now silence! Such silence! Two thousand lay
    dead

In a crescent outside! And within? Not a breath

Save the gasp of a woman, with gory gashed
    head,

All alone, all alone there, waiting for death;

And she but a nurse. Yet when shall we know

Another like this of the Alamo?

Shout "Victory, victory, victory ho!"

I say 'tis not always to the hosts that win!

I say that the victory, high or low,

Is given the hero who grapples with sin,

Or legion or single; just asking to know

When duty fronts death in his Alamo.

**Scheme used: Epizeuxis**—repeating a word or phrase emphatically for effect

Remember how Whitman used epizeuxis in "Oh Captain, My Captain" to change the whole mood, tone, and style? Joaquin Miller uses it in the same way in "Defense of the Alamo." Through the first half of the poem, Miller describes a tragic tale of defeat. Then, shockingly, he yells out, "victory, victory, victory ho!" and transitions to a tale of victory over sin.

Drawing Practice

## "Aedh wishes for the Cloths of Heaven" by William Butler Yeats (1899)
### *The Wind Among the Reeds*

Had I the heavens' embroidered cloths,

Enwrought with golden and silver light,

The blue and the dim and the dark cloths

Of night and light and the half light,

I would spread the cloths under your feet:

But I, being poor, have only my dreams;

I have spread my dreams under your feet;

Tread softly because you tread on my dreams.

**Scheme used: Polysyndeton**—adding unnecessary conjunctions between clauses or words

Yeats uses polysyndeton to overwhelm the reader with the greatness of the cloth he would bestow upon his lady, had he the means. This excessive use of "and" in the first five lines contrasts with its total omission in the rest of the poem. Yeats also repeats many words throughout the poem, as if to prove his poverty, for he even possesses few words.

# Drawing Practice

### Excerpt from "The Darkling Thrush" by Thomas Hardy (1900)
#### Published in *The Graphic*, December 1900

*At once a voice arose among*

*The bleak twigs overhead*

*In a full-hearted evensong*

*Of joy illimited;*

*An aged thrush, frail, gaunt, and small,*

*In blast-beruffled plume,*

*Had chosen thus to fling his soul*

*Upon the growing gloom.*

**Scheme used: Consonance**—repeating consonant sounds in adjacent words with different vowel sounds

I'm not even sure how Thomas Hardy thought of this many words with the "l" sound within them. But they are lovely, aren't they? That soft rolling sound of the "l" makes the entire poem seem to roll off the tongue, much like the little bird whose song rolled into the gloom.

# Drawing Practice

### Excerpt from "The Men of the Maine" by Clinton Scollard (1903)
*Ballads of Valor and Victory*
*Words Aptly Spoken: American Documents*

Not in the dire, ensanguined front of war,

Conquered or conqueror,

'Mid the dread battle-peal, did they go down

To the still under-seas, with fair Renown

To weave for them the hero-martyr's crown.

They struck no blow

'Gainst an embattled foe;

With valiant-hearted Saxon hardihood

They stood not as the Essex sailors stood,

So sore bestead in that far Chilian bay;

Yet no less faithful they,

These men who, in a passing of the breath,

*Were hurtled upon death.*

**Trope used: Simile**—explicitly comparing two seemingly different things using "like" or "as"

Clinton Scollard uses simile a little differently in "The Men of the Maine": instead of describing what the men were like, he describes what they were not like. For the majority of this excerpt, Scollard says only that the men of the Maine did not die as the other soldiers who fought and died in battle did, which makes us question why he is writing this poem in the first place! Then, at the end, we discover that the men of the Maine, while they did not die in battle, were no less faithful than their fellow soldiers and that their deaths were no less honorable. Scollard's masterful use of simile adds interest while revealing deep truths about the subject, as you've seen elsewhere in Shakespeare's and Vaughan's poetry.

Drawing Practice

**Excerpt from "Panama" by James J. Roche (1904)**
*Words Aptly Spoken: American Documents*

Here the oceans twain have waited

All the ages to be mated,—

Waited long and waited vainly,

Though the script was written plainly:

"This, the portal of the sea,

Opes for him who holds the key;

Here the empire of the earth

Waits in patience for its birth."

But the Spanish monarch, dimly

Seeing little, answered grimly:

"North and South the land is Spain's;

As God gave it, it remains.

*He who seeks to break the tie,*

*By mine honor, he shall die!"*

**Trope used: Personification**—ascribing human characteristics to inanimate objects or abstract qualities

You may have noticed that oceans can't wait, since they aren't people, but Roche makes them wait for quite a long while in this poem anyway. The two oceans "waited long and waited vainly" to be joined by the Panama Canal (finally completed in 1914, ten years after this poem was published). Roche gives human characteristics to the oceans in order to make the reader feel that even the oceans want this canal to succeed, and that the Spanish monarch (King Philip II) was acting unjustly when he stopped the canal from being built in the 16th century. This use of personification heightens the emotional appeal and helps the reader make a personal connection to the centuries-long struggle to build the canal.

Drawing Practice

**EXCERPT FROM "THE LOVE SONG OF J. ALFRED PRUFROCK" BY T.S. ELIOT (1915)**
Published in *Poetry*, June 1915

Let us go then, you and I,

When the evening is spread out against the sky

Like a patient etherized upon a table;

Let us go, through certain half-deserted streets,

The muttering retreats

Of restless nights in one-night cheap hotels

And sawdust restaurants with oyster shells:

Streets that follow like a tedious argument

Of insidious intent

To lead you to an overwhelming question …

Oh, do not ask, "What is it?"

Let us go and make our visit.

**Trope used: Personification**—ascribing human characteristics to inanimate objects or abstract qualities

T.S. Eliot gives human characteristics to the evening scene he describes in this excerpt, taken from the very beginning of "The Love Song of J. Alfred Prufrock." Nights cannot themselves be restless, nor can retreats "mutter," but using personification in such a subtle way allows Eliot to inscribe life and personality into the setting of his poem, and to create a mood that permeates all the lines that follow. He also gives the reader a glimpse into the way that the character speaking in the poem sees the world around him, connecting us more deeply to his feelings of restlessness and sadness.

Drawing Practice

## "Trades" By Amy Lowell (1917)
### *Pictures of the Floating World* (1919)

I want to be a carpenter,

To work all day long in clean wood,

Shaving it into little thin slivers

Which screw up into curls behind my plane;

Pounding square, black nails into white boards,

With the claws of my hammer glistening

Like the tongue of a snake.

I want to shingle a house,

Sitting on the ridgepole in a bright breeze.

I want to put the shingles on neatly,

Taking great care that each is directly between

two others.

I want my hands to have the tang of wood:

Spruce, cedar, cypress.

I want to draw a line on a board with a flat pencil.

And then saw along that line,

With the sweet-smelling saw-dust piling up in a yellow heap at my feet.

That is the life!

Heigh-ho!

It is much easier than to write this poem.

**Scheme used: Asyndeton**—omitting necessary conjunctions between clauses or words

In the first stanza, Amy Lowell does not use any conjunctions, making the lines move quickly and fluidly. She also omits the "and" in the following stanza when listing "Spruce, cedar, cypress." The lack of pauses and breaks in these lines mirrors her impatience as she considers the ideal life of the carpenter. The last line of the poem—"It is much easier than to write this poem"—reveals what she's really been trying to rush through: the task of finishing her poem.

## Drawing Practice

## "The Second Coming" by William Butler Yeats (1919)
### Published in *The Dial*, November 1920

Turning and turning in the widening gyre

The falcon cannot hear the falconer;

Things fall apart; the centre cannot hold;

Mere anarchy is loosed upon the world,

The blood-dimmed tide is loosed, and everywhere

The ceremony of innocence is drowned;

The best lack all conviction, while the worst

Are full of passionate intensity.

Surely some revelation is at hand;

Surely the Second Coming is at hand.

The Second Coming! Hardly are those words out

When a vast image out of Spiritus Mundi

Troubles my sight: somewhere in sands of the

   desert

A shape with lion body and the head of a man,

A gaze blank and pitiless as the sun,

Is moving its slow thighs, while all about it

Reel shadows of the indignant desert birds.

The darkness drops again; but now I know

That twenty centuries of stony sleep

Were vexed to nightmare by a rocking cradle,

And what rough beast, its hour come round at

*last.*

*Slouches towards Bethlehem to be born?*

**Scheme used: Polyptoton**—including multiple words that share the same root

Yeats uses polyptoton in the second line, "The falcon cannot hear the falconer," to emphasize the feeling of "turning and turning" from the previous line, for the last word "falconer" turns back to the first word "falcon." This is just one example among many of Yeats's masterful use of form and content to express an idea.

# Drawing Practice

## "The Road Not Taken" by Robert Frost (1915)
### *Mountain Interval* (1916)

Two roads diverged in a yellow wood,

And sorry I could not travel both

And be one traveler, long I stood

And looked down one as far as I could

To where it bent in the undergrowth;

Then took the other, as just as fair,

And having perhaps the better claim,

Because it was grassy and wanted wear;

Though as for that, the passing there

Had worn them really about the same,

And both that morning equally lay

In leaves no step had trodden black.

Oh, I kept the first for another day!

Yet knowing how way leads on to way,

I doubted if I should ever come back.

I shall be telling this with a sigh

Somewhere ages and ages hence:

Two roads diverged in a wood, and I—

I took the one less traveled by,

And that has made all the difference.

**Scheme used: Epanalepsis**—repeating a word or words at the beginning and end of a phrase or clause (broadly–a refrain)

Robert Frost repeats the opening line, "Two roads diverged in a wood" (although slightly altered the second time) at the beginning and end of the poem. He does so to add emphasis and draw the reader's attention back to the initial image of the road. Using epanalepsis also creates a sense of conclusion because it sandwiches the poem.

**Nota Bene:** Epanalepsis is most precise and powerful when it is used within a sentence or a phrase, but it can occur further apart, like the refrain in a song, as in this example.

# Drawing Practice

**EXCERPTS FROM "BIRCHES" BY ROBERT FROST (1915)**
*MOUNTAIN INTERVAL* (1916)

One by one he subdued his father's trees

By riding them down over and over again

Until he took the stiffness out of them,

And not one but hung limp, not one was left

For him to conquer. He learned all there was

To learn about not launching out too soon

And so not carrying the tree away

Clear to the ground. He always kept his poise

To the top branches, climbing carefully

With the same pains you use to fill a cup

Up to the brim, and even above the brim.

Then he flung outward, feet first, with a swish,

Kicking his way down through the air to the ground.

So was I once myself a swinger of birches.

And so I dream of going back to be.

It's when I'm weary of considerations,

And life is too much like a pathless wood

Where your face burns and tickles with the cobwebs

Broken across it, and one eye is weeping

From a twig's having lashed across it open.

I'd like to get away from earth awhile

And then come back to it and begin over.

May no fate willfully misunderstand me

And half grant what I wish and snatch me
    away

Not to return. Earth's the right place for love:

I don't know where it's likely to go better.

I'd like to go by climbing a birch tree,

And climb black branches up a snow-white
    trunk

Toward heaven, till the tree could bear no
    more,

But dipped its top and set me down again.

That would be good both going and coming back.

*One could do worse than be a swinger of birches.*

**Trope used: Onomatopoeia**—using words whose sound echoes the sense of the word

Many poets like using onomatopoeia because of how well it makes the reader imagine a sound and image together. Think of animal sounds. Any time we say the sound an animal makes, we use onomatopoeia. For instance, we use words such as "bark," "meow," and "moo." Saying these words makes us hear the sound. Frost uses the word "swish" in the second stanza to paint a clearer image of swinging on birches.

Drawing Practice

## Excerpt from "Dulce et Decorum Est" by Wilfred Owen (1920)
### *Poems*

If in some smothering dreams you too could pace

Behind the wagon that we flung him in,

And watch the white eyes writhing in his face,

His hanging face, like a devil's sick of sin;

If you could hear, at every jolt, the blood

Come gargling from the froth-corrupted lungs,

Obscene as cancer, bitter as the cud

Of vile, incurable sores on innocent tongues,—

My friend, you would not tell with such high zest

To children ardent for some desperate glory,

*The old Lie: Dulce et decorum est*

*Pro patria mori.*

**Scheme used: Alliteration**—repeating consonant sounds, often at the beginning of words

In this disturbingly vivid poem, Owen masterfully incorporates alliteration by repeating the "w" sound in the lines, "Behind the wagon that we flung him in, And watch the white eyes writhing in his face." I dare you not to imagine this wagon with the man's white eyes writhing! While you may wish to avoid doing so, Owen refuses to let you ignore this image by drawing attention to it through the repetition of the "w" sound.

Also, notice a "w" word he omitted? The topic of the poem begins with a "w," but is never stated: war. Here again we see the power of alliteration to draw an unstated comparison: Owen never has to say the word "war" because his use of alliteration brings it to mind.

Drawing Practice

*Additional products from*

## Classical Christian Education Made Approachable

As a modern parent, are you intimidated at the prospect of building a classical, Christian education for your family? Let this booklet show you a blueprint for the tools of learning! Learn how you too can build your family's home-centered, classical education using the building blocks of knowledge, understanding, and wisdom.

## Classical Acts & Facts History Cards

Classical Conversations has developed its own timeline of 161 historical events, representing major cultures on every continent. The events are divided into seven ages and produced as cards similar to our Classical Acts & Facts Science Cards, with the event title on the front and a fuller description of the event on the back. Each card front also contains a beautiful memory peg image. Images were chosen to serve families all the way through cultural studies in the upper levels of Challenge. The back of each card also includes a world map, pinpointing the event location, and a general timeline, illustrating when the event occurred relative to known history.